I0421640

Greenification

Develop, Educate and Promote

Nurbek Achilov

First Edition

Published in Amazon.com

Nurbek Achilov
Greenification: Develop, Educate and Promote

1st Edition
All Rights Reserved
ISBN: 9781079971255

Table of Content

Introduction

Today, we talk a lot about green development. At the same time, we can see many cars on the streets and we see how they pollute our environment with harmful gases. We can continue the list of negative effects of economic activity and find many reasons that we have to greenify our environments.

However, at the same time, we cannot see practical changes. Governments are busy with resolving many other social issues, businesses are focused on their production and marketing efficiency, people are in deep thinking with their everyday concerns and children are neither can understand nor take actions themselves.

The main point of why we are careless to our environment I concluded in the situation that we can still breathe an air and have something to eat for every day. We also have our shelters where we can come every night after work, eat and rest for a whole night.

Once I was brainstorming and imagined how the world can change in 50 years, when we will be out of water or lack of oxygen because of hot weather conditions, which will last all year around.

So, the idea came to write a book about greenification, a term which should be explained in detail. And it is about how we can develop, educate and promote ourselves to support our global green life.

The book aims to explain the greenification with main definitions and why they are important and how we can start our mind change for more actions.

We are still not late, but it can be late in 20-30 years.

Dedication

This book is for everyone, young and old, rich and poor, healthy and sick, able-bodied and handicap.

And the purpose of the book is to help a reader to change his mind and support humanity for promoting greenification around the world.

A reader can recommend this book for those who are too busy to read or retell the book to friends and colleagues.

Why topic is so important?

We have to accept that we are living with our own glasses, which close our eyes from what is really happening with our nature.

And let us start our brainstorming about what the main events which happening in our world today.

First, our emissions from cars are so huge that now people live under harmful clouds of gasses. At past, we used horses instead of cars and humans were sturdy physically as they breathed clear air. Today, almost in all parts of the world, we have lung problems, which are weakening human body, and as result, to bring healthy offspring.

Second, our emissions from factories are also enormous that we live under chemical clouds. At past, people worked hard by hands and legs to get their products, prey or food. But we believe now that we work smartly in factories or plants. And everything is ok. But it is not.

Third, many people and companies throw their waste or garbage everywhere and carelessly. That's how in many places around the world the underwaters are so polluted with chemicals or heavy metals. And many people, who live in the far regions do not know and drink this water without filtration. Because, they simply do not know and nobody informs them about the water contamination.

As a result, in many places of the world, we have a high level of cancer and other diseases related to the quality of water.

Fourth, we throw our garbage or waste into the oceans, lakes and rivers. In many parts of the world, lakes and oceans are so polluted that you can find no fish in the waters anymore. And it is a main source of food for many countries, especially, near waters with high density of population.

Fifth, in many parts of the world, farmers use many types of chemicals and GMO to increase their productiveness. However, they do not know the long-term effects of what they are growing. And we do not know if they know about the GMO or chemicals at all.

Sixth, the planet has limited resources, but population according the United Nations is increasing, especially in South-East Asia, Africa and Latin America. So, the planet needs more water, food, cloth and resources to provide people with basic products. And, they are delivered from other parts of the planet. As a result, in some parts of the world countries excessively use their water resources, apply chemicals and GMO for increasing the productivity of crops and plants etc.

Seventh, we are becoming observers of started catastrophic changes in the world such as dried out Aral see, melting of glaciers in the mountains, the Arctic and the Antarctica, flooding of vast areas and fires of forests. First time in many centuries, we are having extreme temperature fluctuations on our Earth in the last decade.

Our nature, which existed for thousands of years in a different condition is gradually turning to a new extreme condition for living and surviving of human beings.

Only via greenification and common actions can we able to stop this process gradually. And this book is my starting point to explain.

Structure of the Book

I was asking many times myself how to structure the topic that it will become an interesting topic for all specialists.

Another question was about how to write a book that it will be easy to read for 5-year-old child, who is starting his world and 50 years old professional, who knows a lot, but have less understanding and action to change his behavior, thinking and living for greenification.

The third question was how to make a book adaptable to various countries, which have different level of understanding global issues, recycling or waste management.

And final question was about where to start and how to finish a book so that a reader will gradually build a new thinking and motivation to make own contribution for greenification around the world.

The outline started as follows:

1) My understanding about greenification;
2) My Green Rules;
3) Green City;
4) Green Platforms;
5) Green Policy;
6) Green Culture;

7) Green Management.

As you can see, there are many points to cover in this book. Generally, greenification is complex topic and it will be hard to explain without broader understanding of the world issues.

Let's start from understanding basic things, ideas and concepts.

My understanding about greenification

It will be not strange if you do not find the term and meaning for the word "greenification" in the dictionaries. It is quite new indeed.

30-40 years back nobody was really thinking about the greenification. Years and centuries ago, people were living with their struggles and fights for land, resources and other material world, within specific territories.

Global issues such as greenification were far from imaginations. Even though, there were scientists and experts who were trying to explore the Earth as a planet, for centuries ago.

In an online dictionary at www.definithing.com, I could find the term for greenification. And it explained as follows:

"the networking art of converting what was an untrusted security zone to a trusted zone (aka. green zone)."

It is indeed not clear and one can confuse by reading this term. I thought maybe this is the reason about why we have to understand the term first.

Therefore, it is important to start with defining the term - "greenification".

So, let me here define the word greenification in very simple words. It actually how I understand and define this word.

So, Greenification is a process, which aims to create an environmentally and ecology friendly area with no negative effect for human beings, animals, plants at present and in the future.

It means that greenification aims to create a "green" zone for every living being in our planet, adapting it to the changes and outcomes of the human activity.

Here, it is important to understand that humans need:

-air to breath and live;

-land to survive and work;

-water to drink, plant and support life;

-food to eat and stay strong;

-a living place to sleep and rest;

-health to live and bring offspring;

All these elements require certain conditions that help human beings to live and continue their life.

It requires also certain abilities and skills such as:

-an ability to educate themselves and others to avoid mistakes;

-research new areas to create opportunities and innovations;

-physical work or exercises to preserve genes strong;

-a job to get and save money for better services;

-communication skills with others to transform the knowledge and experience in the best way.

Absence of one element can destroy the whole system or environment easily. And it is a process of greenification that allows to preserve a natural environment for living of human beings.

Indeed, greenification means greenify one area or condition that create better and healthy state for living.

Another point, we have to understand that we can greenify almost everything, including:

1) Environment;
2) Oceans;
3) Rivers;
4) Buildings;

5) Transport;
6) Infrastructure;
7) Houses;
8) Streets and Walking Areas;
9) Roofs;
10) Rooms;
11) Food products;
12) And many other.

The list can continue further, but let's focus on important points.

In order to move greenification in any area, we need the following:

- Resources, which is limited in nature. For example, we are lack of land, fertilizers, materials, raw etc.
- Specialists, who need to be educated and trained appropriately;
- Technologies for management, efficiency and control;
- Investment which is not easy to attract without proper planning and repay;
- Public, which have to be informed and motivated for greenification and purchasing green products and services;
- Standards to ensure quality, measurement and convenience of operations.

In addition, there are many specific areas that should be evaluated in order to start greenification process.

For example, if we take construction of buildings, we have to consider many elements to change and adapt them to our green concept. The most importantly, we have to be sure that at the end the whole building meets the requirements of the standards.

Imagine, if we use the best green technology for external decoration, and at the same time, we use an outdated system of ventilation from the past. The green concept simply will not work for a building.

Therefore, in each and every area, we have to have certain green rules to follow every day.

My Green Rules

According to Cambridge Dictionary, a rule refers to an accepted code or instruction that orders the work in the proper way or should be followed, and shows what is allowed or are not allowed to do.

Definitely, rules depend on many factors and applications for greenification.

In this book, I decided to take the rules from my own experience. Rules that I keep myself and teach my children and people around.

It is clear that construction rules are more specific than my rules.

Anyway, for simplicity, let me write down my main green rules to give a feeling of them:

Rule 1: Do not throw garbage everywhere. It is important to take and separate the garbage and throw it in the proper bin or container.

In some countries, you have to pay for your garbage or sack, in some countries you will get paid for your garbage. Therefore, check your garbage pricing in the local government administration.

Rule 2: Use water sparingly when washing, bathing, brushing teeth etc.

I used to keep water running while I was brushing my teeth, for example, when I was a kid. Today, I teach kids turn off the water in the tap so they have to save clean water and also money for the family.

Rule 3: Use electricity wisely.

Usually at home and in the office, I can see situations that lights, TVs, computers, air conditioners and phones are turning on at the same time.

And sometimes, I notice that my colleagues or kids are sleeping while everything is on.

It is important to ask and teach them to use wisely the electricity and turn off all appliances or equipment which is not used. For example, I also teach my kids to prioritize their usage of various appliances and equipment.

Rule 4: Use effectively computer and photo to save paper efficiently.

Today, in every home or office, we have printers and packs of paper. And usually, our staff or kids use paper without control, printing pictures, photos, texts, tales etc. But at the same time, they use printed material rarely or throw them often to the bin.

And in many cases, I was seeing full baskets of printed paper after the work day or at weekends.

So, it is important in this case to teach staff or your kids how to work on computer, for example, save a file or document in the computer and use it later if required. In this case, there is no need for printing the material.

Rule 5: Promote green ideas and innovations.

Previously, I was putting a like button for a nice message or news, which were describing green innovation or new trend in the market.

Today, I share it in my Facebook, Twitter, LinkedIn, WhatsApp Groups promoting the best green ideas and innovations to as many people as possible.

That's how I can see many new trends not only in my country, but also in my city.

Generally, when you share, you let many people know about the trends and innovations so that they can learn also and change their minds.

Rule 6: Use public transport more often than private car.

Several years ago, I sold my new car. I decided to use public transport and save for investing without a car.

I calculated and understood that a new car strongly influenced my budget, especially with so many traffic jams on the city streets.

I also understood that I was polluting an environment with my car.

So, I decided to use public transport till the time I will buy an electric car.

Rule 7: Collaborate with Green Experts

Many great ideas come when you talk with green experts. Especially, if you are an amateur in the green concepts.

Experts can help to find a right angle or point to start your green action or a new green project. Based on many new concepts you can decrease any risk of being out of the business or the project.

Rule 8: Support Green Projects.

In the period of great changes, we can see many green initiatives in the economy. For example, in Kazakhstan, Coalition for Green Economy and G-Global Development and Association for Ecological Organizations take an important role in realization of various green projects.

In addition, many projects are realized on the regional level, for example, projects for launching solar, wind and hydro energy, waste stations or water supply canals.

International organizations such as the World Bank, European Bank for Reconstruction and Development, Asian Development Bank and many others have their own green projects. To illustrate, the World Bank's portfolio has over 45 projects with total sum exceeding USD 8 billion in Kazakhstan. One of its 3 key strategies in the country is to achieve ecologically sustainable growth and energy efficiency.

For example, the World Bank completed the 17 million-dollar project on Environmental restoration of Ust-Kamenogorsk city, the most polluted city in the region and 30-million-dollar project on forest conservation and increase in areas near pre-Irtysh river zone and Aral Sea, which almost disappeared from the map.

And it is important to support such organizations in project realizations. They also need many expertise and competences to make their projects successful.

Rule 9: Plant Trees annually.

Every spring and autumn are a good time to plant trees. The more you plant, the more you provide an earth with a source of oxygen.

In our family, it is like a tradition to plant trees. And when we talk about tradition it is very useful for our kids who learn a lot to continue this forever.

It takes many years to grow a tree. Some trees you remember with dignity and proud when you see how they grow far to the sky.

This provides some inner energy to do your best and continue your tradition every year.

Rule 10: Buy Green Food.

Demand create supply. If people buy green food often, it will increase supply.

It is important to understand that green food can be classified as follows:

-processed food which do not contain GMO and pesticides;

-fresh food, including fruits and vegetables.

By buying green food, I try to support our real and hardworking farmers.

Rule 11: Invest in Green Technology and Gadgets

Without investment in green technology and gadgets it is impossible to attract masses of people.

They are simply too busy in resolving their social and economic needs every day. Usually, they do not have time even for TV news or promotion information about greenification.

Therefore, investment is a solution to influence and promote green concepts, technologies and ideas.

These are my 11 rules for every day and they can help anyone to stay focused on greenification.

Day by day, these green rules can strengthen green thinking and help you to achieve new green goals.

It is so necessary to form a green thinking nowadays to continue the tradition of greenification.

Green Thinking

Our thinking is something that helps us to learn, develop and grow, not in terms of muscles, but intellectually.

Thinking is an inner process of human brain for managing thoughts, ideas and competencies which allows to generate ideas and form a strong character.

We can also see now that critical thinking is a discussion topic number one and in demand in our societies. That's because of technological changes, when people have to know how to effectively work with multiple information and facts to define the true information and real facts, including reasons and consequences of those sources.

Green thinking is not only a process of understanding, analysis and articulation of green concepts, but also a strong attitude of defending ideas and concepts, focusing on long-term results.

For example, some of the green technologies require up to 20 years of research before the actual project can be launched. For example, a project on building alternative energy station based on nuclear energy. Generally, it requires research and preparation of specialists as the first priority. Besides it needs evaluation of all risks and consequences for people and ecology in case of emergency.

Only with strong green thinking is it possible to stop any political decision, which can be brought based on fast data to meet the requirements of the short-term economic indicators.

Generally, thinking is an internal process of finding the best solution for any case. And it develops gradually, over time in certain environment. In fact, it depends on information, education and constant rules, that can strengthen the thinking of a person to act in various hard situations and discussions.

An important factor for developing and improving the thinking is an environment. And our best environment is our cities and villages today.

Green City

City is a place where the most intellectual people are living. They are professional, demanding and are easy to change. And now cities are competing for green and innovative concepts.

In fact, many cities are on their ways of transforming to green cities. Today, we can see many leading green cities. Importantly, they achieved some progress, so that other cities can learn from them.

In regard to Kazakhstan, we have to learn how to compare and apply the best concepts of green cities. For example, traveling and living in Kazakhstan I can see that many of our cities and villages are far back in application of green concepts and technologies.

Green city concept is not new, but at the same time it is complex and time consuming for implementation, especially if you do not have specialists or technologies.

As examples, let me underline some of the main challenging issues of cities, which are still on their way for greenification:

1) Waste or garbage bins in Kazakhstan, for example, are installed everywhere

but most of them are in very dangerous condition. They are one standard bins. You have to throw all the garbage in one bin.

So, there is no separation of garbage required. And that's the point where all problem starts.

2) All city garbage transported into the landfills without separation and burying. And that's the point of smelly air and polluted areas in regions. In windy days, all light parts of the garbage roll and fly to the far distances spreading the garbage and unpleasant smell.

3) Many cities and almost all villages have no canalization and drainage systems in Kazakhstan. So, it is one of the reasons why we can see the spread of various insects and unpleasant smell in regions.

4) There are many cities and villages which has no trees or flowers in the streets. The reasons can be an absence of a water supply system.

It is also a main reason of lack of sanitation in regions.

5) Electricity supply is one of the main problems for development in many parts of the world.

At the same time, regions are far from installing solar or wind panels or heaters on the roofs of their houses even in situations, when the regions have the greatest number of sunny days.

6) In very hot or cold countries, there is no walking areas for pedestrians. For example, no shelter from a burning summer sun or winter snowfalls.

   Cities do not invest in underground passages or cities where people can walk and do business regardless of the weather condition.

7) In many cities we can daily see a long traffic jams, which pollute and heat the environment.

   There is no system for analyzing their effects. Or no interest for building smart road infrastructure, increasing public transportation or roads for pedestrians and bicycles.

8) In many cities, even in the developed countries, you cannot walk in the streets. They are dirty and soiled by homeless or citizens.

   Even though infrastructure and all signs are available, including for WC.

   So, it is a cultural issue and lack of attitude of people, who needs to be educated.

The good example about cities that they are implementing smart, eco and green concepts all together. So, it is even more challenging topic, but at the same time, it can manage available resources more efficiently, especially for greenification of cities.

There are many issues indeed. And the purpose of this book is to show an idea of how big the topic is for developing cities.

And it is clear that we need many platforms to bring people for constant education and increasing their skills to support greenification.

Green Platforms

Platform are the medium where green experts or state members can transfer their knowledges and skills to the public, citizens and youth.

Many believe that platforms are created only in forums, conferences and round tables or online.

But let's classify platforms below for more clear idea of opportunities for greenification:

1) Events;
2) Educational Centers;
3) Research Centers;
4) Kindergarten;
5) Secondary Schools;
6) Universities;
7) Companies and organizations;
8) Online Portals;
9) Social Media;
10) Call center;
11) Books;
12) Mobile Applications etc.

So, there are a lot of platforms for spreading the idea of greenification. And, it is important to use them effectively.

In many cases from my experience in Kazakhstan, we can see that only events, educational centers and social media are used to transfer green concepts to people.

This is one of reasons why we have so many sceptics about green development in the country.

Moreover, many people understand greenification as a way to withstand a climate change only.

And actually, only via green platforms it is possible to bring people for more understanding and education about the greenification, showing people that it is not only about climate change, but rather how to live in safe, comfortable and smart environment, which will benefit for human's health and activities.

Motivating people and building green infrastructure and platforms requires a lot of efforts, work and investments. And it is important how our policies are working.

Green Policy

Today people think that the greenification is a responsibility of international organizations such as the United Nations, World Bank or governments. It is our psychology and attitudes that we had built at schools and universities and also in our families.

However, greenification is a responsibility of all.

No matter of your position, social status, age or interests. And that's about policy, for example, which should be developed to inform people how to handle waste, invest in green projects or behave in our environment.

A good policy takes a lot of resources to build. And it is important to involve in policy development people from all social groups and ages.

Generally, any green policy should focus on development of rules, procedures, actions and allocation of budget. Taking into account that greenification is non-standard and creative process, it should focus in addition on:

1) Right learning behavior;
2) Growing beneficial relationships;
3) Building positive attitudes;
4) Forming long-term and creative thinking.

For example, let me make a comparison.

Let's take a smart road infrastructure. If we look at it, we can see that there are clear procedures and standards for building roads or data collection. In addition, we have enough specialists, researchers and technologies in the market. So, we have to develop rules, procedures and allocate a budget to build a new road.

On the other hand, a greenification project has no certain accepted rules or standards about what is the best green project for the city. And many achievements will depend on many other factors, and mainly on citizens.

Therefore, policies should focus on people, so that they will not cheat or infringe green rules, for example, throw garbage without separation. People have to be trained and build a strong positive attitude to separate the garbage and throw it in certain bins.

Therefore, policy development requires adaptation and should include educational programs on building attitudes and new skills.

It is also about culture which needs transformation.

To illustrate, those who have never used a waste bins will be shocked to see many types of garbage bins in the streets. Without education and transformation of culture, they will not perceive the bins something important. They will be not be motivated to separate the garbage as they will see it as time-consuming or unnecessary. And wealthy people in some countries might even think that it is not their work at all. Rather they will think that it is a work of service people.

That's shows that policy development should include the following elements as a priority:

1) Education to transform the culture;
2) Responsibility building about environment;
3) Motivation to be a leader in greenification;
4) Supportive subsidies and incentives to make green projects attractive;
5) Green tax schemes for those companies and organizations, which invest in green technologies and innovations;
6) Green certification for quality assurance, motivation and constant improvements;
7) Green awards for motivation of people and leaders of businesses and governments for proactive actions etc.

Generally, right policies will help to form right culture for greenification.

Green Culture

Green Culture is a final step to achieve and transform our present multiple cultures, so that we will never ever destroy our environment, surroundings and save it clean and healthy for our future generations.

We know that today we have thousands of outdated traditions, customs and rules related to our religions, cultures or nationalities.

For centuries they were separating humans and destroying our environments via expansion of territories, uncontrollable use of natural resources, wars, unhuman actions, nuclear or chemical tests etc.

Today, we have global cultures but without unity and wisdom that our planet is a single place and for single common culture.

And we can save our planet for future generations only if we understand that we are a single nation on earth with single culture, traditions and actions to withstand any global threat, war or natural disaster.

Building a green culture can be a starting pillar for uniting our nations for common actions to greenify our world.

From observation of global trends and interests of people to drive cars or use other global brands, it is clear that people all over the world are with the same comfort preferences, tastes and ambitions.

People in different parts of the world are living with same standards for brands, time and scientific innovations.

However, when it comes to water supply, waste management, alternative energy sources, people cannot manage and develop them in the same way in different parts of the world. Even though we have all resources and knowledges, for example, on the internet.

And the main issue is in green management.

Green Management

Previously people thought that a king or leader is a main person who decides what to do in the territory that everybody should follow. Unfortunately, it continues the same in many authoritarian and undeveloped countries.

People are waiting their leaders or kings.

The main difference of the developed countries, which lead the world in greenification of their economies, are in the management structures. Leading countries and organizations provide responsibility, prepare and motivate managers to implement green projects by effectively involving resources, specialists and processes. That is a way how countries achieve better results in greenification.

But in many developing countries, including in Kazakhstan, leaders appoint top managers based on long-term relationships, family interests and individual benefits, and mainly without selection of competitive managers.

That's why many managers in Kazakhstan are fail to do their projects or can show their results only on the paper.

For example, in Kazakhstan, we have promoted green topics over 10 years and linked the best green experts with the local governors and managers. However, till now, many projects realized only with the support of international organizations and companies. There are not many projects with only government or state company participation.

And this is the strong point to show that our governors and state managers are the main barrier in realization of green projects.

For effective green management, it is important to do the following activities:

1) Develop a selection system of cadre based on competitiveness of governors and managers;
2) Train governors and managers to achieve positive outcomes;
3) Send governors and managers abroad for trainings and technology transfer;
4) Delegate roles for governors and managers to play a leading role in their teams;
5) Develop action plans for governors and managers with key indicators to achieve green goals;
6) Build management teams in different parts of the country to achieve regional green goals;

7) Recruit and hire competitive managers who can lead and realize ambitious plans in different levels of management;
8) Share best management practices with other teams and regions;
9) Continue privatization of state companies.
10) Involve international managers to support the green projects.

Ask yourself

After reading the sections above analyze yourself and what you think about the greenification, answer yourself to the following questions:

1) Have I learned greenification issues and topics?
2) Am I ready to support green projects and greenification?
3) Do I have right skills and competences to participate in greenification?
4) Do I have management skills to run a green project?
5) Where to start my green project? And who can help me to realize a project?
6) What are the main platforms to learn green concepts and find green experts?
7) What are the new green rules I have to practice every day?
8) Are there any new policies that we should develop to support greenification?

List of Main Green Organizations in Kazakhstan

1) Coalition for Green Economy and G-Global Development
   Web-site: www.greenkaz.org
2) Association of Ecological Organizations in Kazakhstan
   Web-site: www.aeok.kz
3) ROP Operator
   Web-site: www.recycle.kz

List of Global Green Organizations

1) United Nations Environment Programme
   Web-site: www.unenvironment.org
2) European Environment Agency
   Web-site: www.eea.europa.eu
3) Intergovernmental Panel on Climate Change
   Web-site: www.ipcc.ch
4) Global Green Growth Institute
   Web-site: www.gggi.org

Conclusion

This book is the beginning point of disclosure of key topics of our economies on building and promoting greenification.

It is our aim to save our planet and greenify it for healthy and long-lasting happiness of people and future offspring.

And there are a lot of to do in many parts of our world.

As an author I will be happy to see your comments and ideas about how I can improve my next editions of this book and important issues of today's global agenda.

Feel free send me your message or your comment via email at: innoker@gmail.com

About author

Nurbek Achilov is a global citizen with more than 10 years of experience in research of waste management and alternative energy sources. He is involved as a lecturer of marketing and management at the South-Kazakhstan State University.

Nurbek enjoys writing about multiple issues of the green economy and development. As a member of educational institutions, he understands well about the problems of greenification. He explores many areas on how to develop our green and smart economy.

Notes and Memories

Where can you find interesting stories about investments, export and trade on the internet?

Nurbek Achilov has some resources for you!

On Blogger's platform he runs his blog about investments, export, trade and other issues.

Blog about investment, export and trade in English:

https://nurbekachilov.blogspot.com/

Blog about investment, export and trade in English:

https://nurbekachil.blogspot.com/

You can also find ideas, photos and experiences about investments, trade and investment on Nurbek Achilov's pages in Facebook, Instagram, Pinterest, Slideshare,

Academia and LinkedIn and other accounts.

orcid.org/0000-0003-1238-6556

Kazakhstan

Tips for Travelers

Nurbek Achilov

Second Edition

Get my new book with the Special Price on
Amazon.com

---

*200 web-sites
and tools for
online presence*

Essential Handbook for marketing and growth

Nurbek Achilov

First Edition

Event Management

Tips and strategies

Nigel Aksel

Second Edition

Global Citizen

Thinking Beyond

Nurbek Achilov

First Edition